Finding Out About
VICTORIAN TOWNS

Michael Rawcliffe

Batsford Academic and Educational Ltd *London*

—Contents—

Typeset by Tek-Art Ltd, London SE20
and printed in Great Britain by
R.J. Acford
Chichester, Sussex
for the publishers
Batsford Academic and Educational Ltd,
an imprint of B T Batsford Ltd,
4 Fitzhardinge Street
London W1H 0AH

ISBN 0 7134 4289 1

ACKNOWLEDGMENTS

The author wishes to thank the Sheffield Library and the Bromley Library for their help in preparing this book.

The author and publishers would like to thank the following for their kind permission to reproduce copyright illustrations: Birmingham Reference Library, pages 42, 43; W. Eglon Shaw, the Sutcliffe Gallery, page 24; Heart of England Newspapers Ltd, Leamington Spa, page 34 (bottom); St John's House, Warwick (Warwickshire Museum), page 34 (top); Sheffield City Museums, page 11. Illustrations on pages 3, 7, 9, 13, 20-21, 22, 23, 28, 29, 30-31, 32, 38 and 41 are from the author's collection. Pictures on pages 8, 12, 18, 33 and 37 are from the publishers' collection. The map on page 45 was drawn by Rudolph Britto. The plan on page 14 was taken from *The Making of the English Landscape* by W.G. Hoskins (Hodder, 1977).

The songs included in the book were taken from *A Touch of the Times*, edited by R. Palmer (Penguin, 1974).

Introduction

Today the majority of us live in towns or cities. This has not always been so. In 1801 seven out of ten people lived in the country, but by 1901 only two. Today few people live far away from an urban area and most of us have probably visited several of the larger ones.

This book is about Victorian towns, and you will quickly see that a town in 1837 was very different from the same town at the end of Victoria's reign in 1901. You have only to consider the changes which you yourself have seen: the shops that have changed hands, the increasing problem of the motor car and parking, the building of a new supermarket or even a new pedestrian precinct, to realize how quickly change takes place. This book is concerned with the enormous changes which occurred in the nineteenth century during the long reign of Queen Victoria (1837-1901).

During the nineteenth century the population of England and Wales grew very rapidly, rising from nearly nine million in 1801 to thirty-five million a hundred years later. The biggest increase took place in the larger towns and cities, which rapidly expanded as a result

Gustave Doré's impression of Ludgate Circus in the 1860s. Note the horse-drawn omnibuses and the out-passengers on top.

of the spread of railways in the 1840s. This was only ten years after the opening of the Liverpool-Manchester Railway in 1830 — the first to link two of our major cities. One writer at the time said:

It was only yesterday but what a gulf between then and now. Then was the old world [of] stage coaches, pack horses . . . . We who lived before railways are like Father Noah and his family out of the Ark.

I wonder what changes in the twentieth century have had as great an effect?

As more people flocked to the towns, so there was increased overcrowding in the poorer areas and various dangers to health were caused through impure drinking water, poor drainage and the lack of sewage disposal. Frequently people resented being compelled to conform to bye-laws, or having to pay rates towards improvements. Fever and disease often grew worse before any action was taken. Remember, though, that improvement for one may mean loss to another. The building of the London railway lines and stations, and the building of Oxford Street, forced many poor families to move into already densely populated slums.

In time, improvements in public health and building did take place and the Victorians came to take great pride in their new town hall, library, covered market or new shopping street.

In this book you will read not only about these changes, but also about the people who lived in those days and the problems and the pleasures which they experienced. Each section of the book can be a starting point for your study. I hope that you will be able to find out more about what your own area was like in Victorian times.

1. PEOPLE

a) Once you have decided what you want to study, go to your main library, to either the reference or the local history section. The librarian will be able to suggest similar materials to the ones mentioned in this book, about your town.

b) The vicar or warden of the local parish church. It is always best to check first to see whether the church or chapel is open and you ought to ask permission if you want to rub any gravestones or work inside the building.

c) There are very few Victorians still living, but old people have lots to tell about their parents' memories and often have old photographs and mementoes which they might show you.

2. THE TOWN ITSELF

There is no substitute for walking round and looking. Start at the railway station or the parish church, finding out when each was built. Then look for other buildings that would have been there at the time (see 3.b.). Many towns have produced their own town walks. Ask the librarian if there is one available.

3. VISUAL MATERIAL

a) *Old photographs* Many local libraries, e.g. Sheffield and Lewisham, have produced sets of postcards from their old photographs, while Pamlin Prints of Croydon (Collector-card, Croydon CR0 1HW) produce them of several areas. Original old photographs of street scenes are becoming more difficult to find, but you may have photographs in family albums which are good for showing us the fashions of the Victorians.

b) *Maps* The Ordnance Survey had produced maps of every part of the country by the middle of the nineteenth century and most areas have at least two large-scale maps at the 6" and 25" to the mile scale. The latter shows clearly the shape of individual buildings and even marks trees and post boxes. Get a copy of the part you are interested in from the library and compare it with the most modern map you can find. Even then you will probably find the modern map out of date when you begin to walk round.

An estate agent may have a modern street map which you will find very useful for its lists of street names.

c) *Prints and paintings* These were the only records before the photograph. They can be very useful, but remember that they may not be completely accurate.

4. WRITTEN SOURCES

a) *Local histories* People have been writing about their area for many years. Even if their records are difficult to read, they may contain some useful photographs.

b) *Victorian guides and directories* These are particularly useful as they were written for use at the time. Kelly's *Post Office Directory* was produced for every county and gives lots of detail of each town and village. Town directories will give even more detail and often give the name of every householder and certainly every street.

c) *Advertisements* Look at those in guides, directories and newspapers. They give lots of detail of shops, holidays and fashion.

d) *Newspapers* Most places had their own local paper in the nineteenth century. These are useful for looking up particular events such as the opening of the new town hall or the Diamond Jubilee Celebrations of 1897.

e) *Documents* These are the working papers of the time, e.g. the school log books, or workhouse diet sheets. Several large schools and libraries have started to produce selections of sources on their local area or on particular

aspects, such as the Market Square.

f) *Diaries or memoirs* A local person may have kept a diary or written down memories of childhood. The local newspaper today often publishes articles on the past.

g) *Census material* The originals are in the new Public Record Office in London, but your local reference library will probably have copies of the entries for your town in the nineteenth century. As census information contains personal details, such as one's age and occupation, it is not made available until 100 years after it was taken. The first census was in 1801, but they are more useful from 1851, when they include each person's place of birth.

5. OBJECTS

These range from seaside souvenirs, e.g. a plate of 1900 showing the Blackpool Tower, to school prizes. When walking around, look out for Victorian post boxes (V.R.), water troughs, drinking fountains and other signs of the Victorian past.

6. STREET AND INN NAMES

Both these give useful clues. The Bricklayers Arms, the Prince Albert, the Railway Signal all tell us something about the time they were built or who used them (not Prince Albert!) You can often date roads by their names, e.g. Jubilee Terrace (1887 or 1897?), Alma Road (battle in the Crimean War), Gordon Road (famous Victorian General).

Industries and Trades

Many new industries and trades grew up during the nineteenth century, while existing ones developed rapidly with the coming of the railway, inventions and the growing demands of the people. Some contemporary writers wrote proudly of these changes. Others were more concerned with what it would have been like to live and work in the towns and factories.

BIRMINGHAM TRADES AND INDUSTRIES

John Wilson, the author of a Gazeteer of England and Wales, published in 1876, wrote:

> The largest establishments are for iron and brass founding; for the rolling, stamping, plating and drawing of metals; for iron roofs and girders, steam engines and railway wagons, lamps and gasometers; galvanized iron and metallic bedsteads; and for glass-blowing, coach making and brewing.

Birmingham was also well-known for the range of its trades, as Wilson and the song that follows indicate. Wilson's Gazeteer said:

> Trades employing large numbers of work people are for tools, machines, steel pens, steel toys, keys, locks, screws, bolts, files, buckles, fire irons, bridle-bits, iron chains, awl-blades, axle trees and nails . . . . The trade in buttons, in buckles and in locks . . . the gun trade . . . glass working, besides plate glass, stained glass, chandeliers, candelabra, lustres and similar objects, produces such things as beads, bugles, buttons, hour glasses and many kinds of toys . . . . Jewellery of all kinds and many sorts of silver and gold toys are made. Papier mâché, enamelled and japanned, is a staple trade. Bone, whalebone, ivory and pearl are largely worked.

You will see several of these items in your local museum or in antique shops. Many of them were made in small workshops. Birmingham was just the place for a man seeking work to go, as shown in this verse from a contemporary song, "Jack of All Trades":

> In Smallbrook Street made candle-sticks,
> In Worcester Street a broker;
> In Floodgate Street made fire-irons,
> Both shovel, tongs and poker.
> In Ann Street was a dialist,
> Newhall Street a die-sinker;
> In New Street drove a hackney coach,
> In Moor Street was a printer.

SHEFFIELD STEEL

Sheffield was famous for its steel. A song, "Sheffield's a Wonderful Town, O", had a verse:

> For cutlery so famed none with Sheffield
>   can be named,
> Where the people all their lives, they
>   make razors, scissors, knives,
> In this very wonderful town, O.
> Lots of files, all in piles;
> Stones go round, razors ground;
> Friday quick goes boring stick;
> Saturday get your pay,
> Then regale yourselves with ale.

The dust from the grindstones was very injurious to health, and the grinders, though well paid, often died in their early 30s.

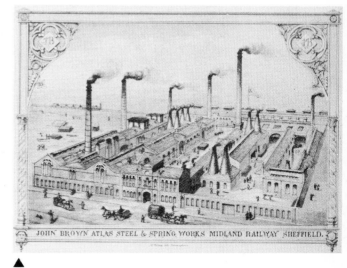

▲ An advertisement for a large Sheffield works. Note the size of the factory and the two forms of transport. The factory has been built on the outskirts of the city.

◄ Green Lane Steel Works, Sheffield. Why do you think the factory entrance was built in such an imposing way?

WOOL AND COTTON

Woollen and cotton manufacture were two of our major industries. A *Pictorial History of Lancashire* includes this description of Bolton in 1844:

> As we approached . . . Bolton steam chimneys arose before us, . . .
>   The principal trade is the cotton manufacture and subsidiary branches of bleaching, calico printing, machine making etc.

If you live in, or near, a cotton town, find out how many of the mills and factories are still in use and what is now being produced in them.

Wilson described Leeds in 1876:

> The cloth manufacture is not confined to any one kind, . . . it produces fabrics equal to the best which were formerly produced in the west of England; . . . it produces also such varieties, from superfine to coarse, from broad to narrow, and from shawl to blanket.

Use guides and directories to find out what your town produced at this time.

—Life in Industries and Trades—

A MANCHESTER MILL

Not everyone admired the growing industries. The Frenchman Taine visited England in 1861 and 1871. He described Manchester in 1861:

> Walked through the city; seen close at hand, it is still more dismal. The air and the soil appear charged with fog and soot. Manufactories with their blackened bricks, their naked fronts, their windows destitute of shutters, and resembling huge and cheap penitentiaries [prisons], succeed each other in rows. . . .
>
> One of these buildings is a rectangle of six stories, in each of which are 40 windows; it is there that, lit up by gas, amid the deafening noise of looms, thousands of work people, cabined, classifiable, immovable, mechanically drive their machines every day from morning to night. . . . About six o'clock a bustling, noisy crowd pours from the mills into the streets; men, women, and children flock along in the open air; their clothes are filthy, many of the children are bare-footed, the faces of all are pinched and gloomy . . .

Why do you think cotton mills (factories) were so large? Find out how young the children would have been.

AN IRON WORKS IN WALES

In South Wales the Dowlais Iron Works had transformed the rural area north of Merthyr. Charles Knight described Merthyr in 1854:

> . . . the whole of this distance is occupied by persons exclusively, or almost exclusively, dependent on the vast iron works of the district. The Dowlais Company owns a vast tract of country, where they mine their own coal, iron and limestone, and cast them into the huge furnaces which yield the molten metal . . . they give occupation to the enormous number of 6,000 persons . . . about a 1,000 tons of coal per day are used at the work.

You can still see the effects of these or later workings in the Welsh valleys and hillsides (see page 41).

Lancashire cotton weaving, c. 1900. Imagine the noise when the machinery was in operation and see how little space there was between the rows of machines.

SEASIDE TOWNS

Seaside towns provided very different occupations. Charles Knight described Margate in 1854:

> As for the natives they are nearly all lodging-house keepers, or letters of lodgings, or bedrooms. They work very hard during the season . . . they cook and do for you. In the larger of the houses, they are incessantly washing shrimps or frying fish, or boiling or roasting. . . . it lasts only four months . . . nay in wet summers often not more than two.
>
> About the middle of September the boats come down almost empty and go back full, and this . . . soon leaves Margate as quiet as a town can be.

Where do you think Margate's visitors mainly came from?

DOMESTIC INDUSTRIES

Many people continued to work at home long after factories were introduced. In 1876 James Thorne described one domestic (home) industry in St Albans, which grew rapidly with the popularity of straw hats and boaters:

> Straw-plaiting is now the staple industry . . . some thousands of hands are employed in the straw trade in the town and the neighbourhood. On a Summer's day almost every house in the back streets may be seen with the street door (opening into the living room) set wide open, and women and girls busy plaiting, and talking and singing . . . or, often, rocking a cradle with the foot, whilst they ply their nimble fingers without ever seeming to look at their work.

Many domestic workers were very poorly paid. Mary Colton was a Nottingham laceworker who started work at the age of 6. In evidence to the Children's Employment Committee in 1842, she described how she now took in work from a lace warehouse in Nottingham and how she had to dose her own young child to keep her quiet, while she got on with her work. She said:

> [I] can earn about 3/- a week now, working from 9 A.M. to 10 P.M. having one hour for dinner and three quarters of an hour for tea.

Do you think that Thorne's account was too rosy in the light of the last extract?

◄ Two coal miners in Wigan, c.1900. Women worked in the coal industry, but in 1842 were forbidden from working underground. Can you suggest two reasons which show that this photograph was posed?

The Family at Home

The Victorian town and city contained a variety of homes and districts and the poor often lived very close to the wealthy, or to the central shopping area. Close to the open space of the Haymarket in Bristol were enclosed courts and covered alleys. James Crosby described the homes there in 1884:

On a dull day, you would pass the narrow, door-like entrance of this alley, without becoming aware of its existence. Entering we find ourselves in a court of six or eight three storey houses . . . . The occupants — labourers, quay rangers, hawkers and men of uncertain employment — would with difficulty be induced to pay more than 1/6d. per week to be "housed" at night. A bedstead without a bed, or . . . a piece of sacking with a bundle of rags on the floor, two shattered chairs, the fragments of a table, and a saucepan are their household goods. The breadwinner goes out in the morning and returns to sleep at night — the children of school age are mercifully looked after by the School Board, . . . while the whole family of five or six live and sleep in one room.

Every town, however small, had its poor. Bromley in Kent, soon to be a prosperous Kent suburb, had several yards just behind the busy Market Square. The Census of 1851 recorded that one house in Old Chapel Yard contained the following people:

Wm. Huggett, labourer and his wife.
A. Hillian and his wife, a washerwoman.
Also nine lodgers who worked as rail labourer (1), shoemaker (4), maker of chair bottoms (1), hawker (1) and two children aged two.

Only three of the adults knew where they had been born.

Fortunately, slums such as this have now been demolished, but the census returns give us detailed information as to who lived in these properties.

THE BETTER-OFF

Contrast the descriptions of the poor with Richard Church's description of his childhood home in the 1890s:

Hitherto I had spent much time in an armchair in the long parlour, front and back rooms thrown into one by opening folding doors.
I never saw these doors closed. The arch above them, and also the two fireplaces, were hung with plush curtains edged with tassels. I remember how carefully I had to move about in the long room, for odd tables, stands, corner shelves, were dotted about, filling the floor space, and displaying a wealth of vases, photograph frames, decorated boxes, folded ivory fans, and convoluted glassware . . . . The space below the bay window in the front was impenetrable being filled with bamboo stands carrying enormous flower-pots, out of which rose a jungle of aspidistras.

Write a similar paragraph describing your living room and its contents. Then compare it with the above.

THE PRINCIPAL PARTS OF A HOUSE IN 1870

Large Victorian houses had a wide variety of rooms. The next extract comes from a book on the design and furnishing of homes for the comfortably off. The author describes the range of rooms — though he adds that, while a mansion would have many more, few houses will have all these.

i *Parts of access and means of communication from one part to another* — 1. Porch or Portico. 2. Entrance hall or lobby. 3. Staircases. 4. Passages.

ii *Ordinary sitting-rooms and reception rooms* — 1. Breakfast, or Morning-room. 2. Dining-room. 3. Drawing-room.

iii *Rooms devoted to special purposes, not generally found in ordinary houses* — 1. Library. 2. Study, or Business-room. 3. Billiard-room. 4. Gallery.

iv *Rooms that have their location in the first or upper floors* — 1. Bedrooms. 2. Dressing-rooms. 3. Lady's Sitting-room. 4. Bathroom.

v *Rooms set apart specially for children* — 1. Day Nursery. 2. Night Nursery. 3. Schoolroom.

vi *Domestic offices of all kinds* — 1. Kitchen. 2. Back Kitchen, or Scullery. 3. Pantry. 4. Larder. 5. China Closet, etc. 6. Cellars for wine, etc. 7. Cellars for Fuel. 8. Waterclosets.

vii *Useful, but not indispensable, adjuncts to a house* — 1. Conservatory. 2. Roof garden. 3. Ice house or Room. 4. Wash-house. 5. Laundry. 6. Brewery. 7. Dairy.

Calculate the number of servants which would be needed to staff such a house. Many of the large Victorian houses have been converted into flats or are being demolished. Why is this? Plans and old photographs can help, and the census returns will give the numbers in the family and of the servants.

The kitchen/living room of the Manager of Abbeydale Works in Sheffield, c. 1890. Note the lighting and the range. Why would kitchen chores have taken longer than today?

Differing Neighbourhoods

THE HORROR OF INDUSTRIAL CITIES

The industrial city came as a shock to many visitors. In the *Pictorial History of Lancashire* one writer described his impressions of Manchester as he approached it by rail in 1844:

> The prospect is anything but cheering. Forests of chimneys, clouds of smoke and volumes of vapour, like the seething of some stupendous cauldron, occupy the entire landscape; there is no sky but a dark gray haze . . . masses of smoke more dense than the rest, which look like fleeces of black wool.

Taine came to a similar conclusion. Here are his comments on the poor and their housing in Manchester, 1861:

> What wretched streets! Through the half open windows may be seen a miserable room on the ground floor, sometimes below the level of the damp pavement; at the thresh-hold a group of white, fat, and untidy children breathe the foul air of the street, less foul, however, than that of the room. A strip of carpet may be perceived, and clothes hung up to dry.

and Liverpool, 1861:

> It is now six o'clock, and we return through the poorer quarter. What a sight! In the vicinity of Leeds Street there are 15 or 20 streets across which cords are stretched and covered with rags and linen, hung up to dry. Bands of children swarm up every flight of steps . . . their faces pale, their light hair in disorder, their clothes are in tatters, they have neither shoes nor stockings, and they are all shockingly dirty . . . . Perhaps nearly 200 children romp and wallow in a single street . . . . What interiors! They contain a little piece of worn oil cloth; sometimes a shell ornament . . . the smell resembles that of an old rag shop . . . . The ground floor of nearly every dwelling is a flagged and damp basement. Can one imagine what life in these cellars must be during the Winter?

Why was the washing hung up across the street? What were the problems of basements or cellars in areas such as this?

The novelists Charles Dickens and Mrs Gaskell both did much to bring the horrors of the industrial city to the attention of their readers.

Those who could afford to lived on the fringes of the city. In the following extract, about Manchester in 1844, see how the city expands and note the result. Victoria Park was on the outskirts of Manchester.

> At Victoria Park, an attempt has been made to combine domestic comfort with architectural taste. The rapid conversion of the private residences in Mosley Street and many other parts induced a company of gentlemen to purchase this park, which contains about 140 acres of land, in order to stud it with villas [close] to the town with a freedom from the smoke of the factories. (From the *Pictorial History of Lancashire*)

Perhaps this was the area of the suburbs which Taine later visited in 1861:

> Hence have been constructed vast silent streets in which there are no shops, and in which each house, surrounded by a patch of green, is detached, and is occupied by a single family. The trim lawns, the small gates . . . the painted fronts . . . make one think of painted menageries and of neat playthings.

◄ *A paved wynd (alley) in Glasgow. The only entrance was through the covered entry from the High Street. Note the height and condition of the buildings and the open drain to the right. (See Dr Arnott's description of Glasgow on page 14.)*

You will be unlikely to find a detailed description of your area, ► *but there will be directories and large-scale Ordnance Survey maps available in your library. This is an extract from the Penge and Anerley section of Burdett's Directory of 1866. You can see the shopkeepers and their trades. How do they compare with your shops? Who do you think lived in the houses with names?*

4	BURDETT & Co.'s DIRECTORY.

ANERLEY ROAD.	ANERLEY ROAD.
75 Park, Robert, *Thicket Hotel*	15 Cannon, R. R., *Grocer*
Here is Thicket Grove.	13 Smith, W., *Greengrocer*
73 Rickett Smith and Co., *Coal Merchants*	11 Branson, G,. *Bootmaker*
71 Moger & Co., *Coal Merchants*	9 Kraus, J. F., *Baker*
The Remainder of this Road is in the Norwood Postal District.	7 & 5 Dakin, H., *Draper*
	3 Palmer, F., *Chemist*
69 Parrish, J., *Hatter*	1 Nottage, Nath., *Brunswick Hotel*
67 Larner, G., *Stationer*	Pass Crystal Palace Station Road.
65 Brooke & Co., J. A., *Dyers*	Porter, D., *Baker*, Red House
63 Goodwin, E. T. ⅼ ., *Photographer*	McLeod, Mrs., Spring Mount
61 Amos & Son, *Pianoforte Ware-house*	Todd, Mrs., Chalwood
59 Evans & Co., *Greengrocers*	Eames, Alfred, The Knoll
57 Holmyard, Mrs., *Juvenile Out-fitter*	Spencer, Mrs., Mount View
	Alexander, Mrs., Peakville
55 Holmyard, J. H., *Draper*	Gould, Mrs., The Summit
53 Bushell, H., *Bootmaker*	— Unoccupied, Redhurst
51 Shiers, M., *Tobacconist*	Smyth, S. J., Keston Lodge
49 Brooker, G., *Ham and Tongue Warehouse*	Herring, Mrs., Hillside
47 Leman, E., *Chemist*	Cole, Alexander, Surrey View
45 — Unoccupied	Tippetts, Mrs., Southbourn
43 & 41 Reynolds, Thomas D. *Fancy Draper*	Hale, Mrs., Rockville
	Bell, Mrs., High View
39 Galton, Dr. J. H., M.D.	Clinton, H. R., Crècy
37 Solman, J., *Corn Merchant and Grocer*	Pass Railway Avenue.
35 — Unoccupied	Crystal Palace School Practical Engineering
	Principal—J. W Wilson, C.E.
	Bertram & Roberts, *Refreshment Contractors*

OVERCROWDED TOWNS

The rapid rise in the population of the towns created dangers to health. The poorest arrivals flocked into the already over-crowded slums where the rents were lowest. Even new housing was badly built, often on poorly drained and cheap land.

The Report of the Health of Towns Commission (1845) shows how short of space Nottingham was:

> I believe that nowhere else shall we find so large a mass of inhabitants crowded into courts, alleys, and lanes as in Nottingham, and those, too, of the worst possible construction. Here they are so clustered upon each other; court within court, yard within yard, and lane within lane, in a manner to defy description . . . . Some parts of Nottingham [are] so very bad as hardly to be surpassed in misery by anything to be found.

FEVER

One of the consequences of the bad housing conditions can be seen in Dr Neil Arnott's description of Glasgow in 1840. He was a physician employed by the Poor Law Commission to carry out enquiries into preventable diseases (fever).

> The great mass of the fever cases occurred in the low wynds [alleys] and dirty narrow streets and courts in which because lodging was there cheapest, the poorest and most destitute naturally had their abodes. From one such locality, between Argyll Street and the river, 754 of about 5,000 cases of fever which occurred in the previous year, were carried to the hospitals.

Unfortunately, it was only after the outbreak of diseases such as cholera and typhus that action was taken. In many areas local boards of health were elected and medical officers of health appointed. There was fever in Stratford-upon-Avon in 1865. By this time a local board of health had been established, and its minutes read:

> It appearing to the Board from the report of two Medical Men to the Board of Guardians that fever is prevalent in the Town, Ordered that notice be given that the Board have directed the Inspector of Nuisances at his discretion to supply any poor person in the District on his or her application with sufficient lime and the

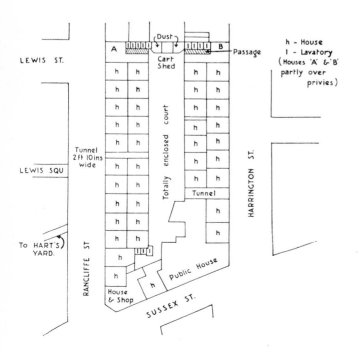

A typical Nottingham court, taken from the Report of the Royal Commission on the State of the Large Towns, 1845. *Note the back-to-back houses (h) and the tunnel through which the court is approached. Housing such as this was the result of the shortage of building land.*

use of a Bucket and Brush free of Cost for the purpose of whitewashing the inside of the dwelling house of such poor person.

What did the Stratford Board hope to achieve by this?

Contrast their official statement with what James Greenwood wrote in *The Wilds of London*, published in 1874. He interviewed the inhabitants of one of London's poorest areas — Turnmill Street Alleys, Clerkenwell — where every room contained a family. Still new families came.

"There have been a thousand houses pulled down for the railway within half a mile of this, and they come swarming down here after lodgings because there's nowhere else to look for 'em."

Why would this make things worse? One inhabitant described what happened when people were "a-dyin' up of fever here like rotting sheep":

"The police came with their chloride of lime and their brushes, and their white-wash pails, and it was 'Move on there' and there wasn't to be no living of two families to a room, nor no chuckin' your waste of vegetables and that into the cellar, when the dust heap was a-runnin' over . . . . Well, what came of it? They whitewashed every mortal *outside* thing they could dab a brush on, and they turned the donkeys out of the parlours . . . then they walked off, and we have seen nothing of 'em since. . . ."

What trade do you think the owners of donkeys followed? How reliable do you think evidence such as this is?

WATER SUPPLY

Greenwood then described the problem of water supply. Note that there were several water companies in London at this time.

There is a cistern attached to each alley, and once every week-day the water company allows a limited supply to run into it.

In this particular area Greenwood estimated that each alley contained on average twenty houses with four families (of five people) in each. There was one outside lavatory per alley. How many people did it serve and what was the main risk to health?

PUBLIC WORKS

Improvements came, but they were gradual and drainage and sewage schemes were expensive. Birmingham was quick to take advantage of the Artisans' Dwelling Act of 1875, which allowed local authorities to compulsorily purchase slum areas and build new houses. No wonder the Victorians came to talk with pride about their public works.

In his Gazeteer of England and Wales, John Wilson described the port of Birkenhead:

A court-house, two banks, gas-works, waterworks, working-men's houses, an abattoir [slaughter-house], and an extensive new cemetery, also draw attention.

Which of these would have helped the health of the people and in what way?

Find out where your water supply comes from and where the sewage works are. When were they first built?

Family Budgets

Various surveys were made from the 1840s onwards, by individuals or groups who were concerned about the plight of the poor. Information about the better off and the rich comes mainly from the growing number of books and articles published at the time. All these showed how families on particular incomes might live.

However, work was not always regular, and during unemployment the family would be dependent on charity or the workhouse. Sickness, the death of the breadwinner, drunkenness or gambling all made life more difficult, if not impossible.

Do not look at these budgets and compare them with prices today. Rather, see what could be bought with the wages at that time.

AN URBAN SEMI-SKILLED WORKER EARNING 15/- A WEEK

This was the budget of a semi-skilled worker in 1841. He had three children.

	s.	d.
5 4lb. loaves at 8½d.	3	6½
5lb. of meat at 5d.	2	1
7 pints of porter (beer) at 2d.	1	2
½cwt. coals		9½
40lbs. of potatoes	1	4
3oz. tea, 1lb. sugar	1	6
1lb. butter		9
½lb. soap, ½lb. candles		6½
Rent	2	6
Schooling		4
Other things		5½
	15	0

(See page 46 for old and new money)

AN OVERLOOKER IN A MANCHESTER COTTON FACTORY

£1 a week for a family of four was probably the dividing line between hunger and subsistence in mid-century. Here is the budget of a skilled worker in 1841. He had several of his six children working and the income per week was £1.14.0.

	£	s.	d.
Rent		5	0
Flour or bread		5	10
Meat 7lb. at 8d.		4	8
Bacon ½lb.			4
Butter 2lb.		2	0
Eggs (18?)		1	0
Milk 8 pints		1	0
Potatoes 40lbs.		1	8
Cheese 1lb.			9
Tea ¼lb.		1	0
Coffee ¼lb.			6
Sugar 3lb.		2	0
Soap 1lb.			6
Candles 1lb.			6
Coals 2cwt.		1	2
	1	7	11

List the ways in which this family is living better than the previous one.

What is missing from this budget? Note that there is virtually nothing to spare.

THE POOREST PEOPLE

Even at the turn of the century many people earned less than the overlooker. Seebohm Rowntree carried out a survey of York in 1899-1900 and found that over a quarter of the people were living in poverty. The poorest had no more than 18/- a week:

> The food of these people is totally inadequate . . . consisting largely of a dreary succession of bread, dripping and tea; bread and butter and tea; bacon, bread, and coffee, with only a little butcher's meat.

Many of these people had to resort to the pawnshops:

> The pawnshop often plays an important part in the lives of the people in the slums. . . . The children are sent off with a weekly bundle early in that day [Monday], and a number of them may sometimes be seen sitting on the steps outside the pawnshop door waiting for it to open. . . . Some families pawn their Sunday clothes every Monday and redeem them as regularly on the following Saturday night when the week's wages have been received.

Do you know what the pawnbrokers' sign was? How do you think the pawnbroker made a living?

A LONDON PRINTER

Not everyone was poor, and many skilled workers were comfortably off. A modern historian, G.M. Young, has described the family of a printer in a London suburb in 1860:

> Now at £3 a week, they have the whole house to themselves and their three children. Meat is 6d. a pound; they can dress themselves in good cloth and sound leather, the father for nine or ten pounds a year, the mother for six or seven pounds, and the children perhaps for two pounds each. He and his wife are really very comfortable.

Before he earned £3 a week, what did the family have to do to pay the rent? (Look at the first sentence.)

THE VERY COMFORTABLY OFF

Mrs Earle in *The Cornhill Magazine* in 1901 shows how a London family with £1,800 a year might spend their money.

	£
Rents, rates and taxes	360
Housekeeping including living, washing, lighting	550
Repairs, including cleaning, painting, etc.	100
Coal	60
Dress (man and woman)	200
Wages, including beer, and four servants	130
Wine	60
Stamps, newspapers, stationery, etc.	30
Doctors, dentists, accidents, journeys	100
New house linen	20
Charities	40
	1,650

Try to find a copy of Mrs Beeton's *Book of Household Management* which was written for wives to show how they should organize their home. It became "the bible" of the better off.

Hard Times

As we have seen, weekly budgets can be very misleading, for work was not always regular. For example, in the days of sail, dockers in London would be without work if the wind prevented ships sailing up the Thames. But there were many different causes of unemployment.

A contemporary drawing of the Monday morning queue outside a pawn shop. Note the range of goods to be pawned and the resigned faces of those queueing.

1842 was a particularly bad year for trade and there was much unemployment, as Harriet Martineau described:

> At *Hinckley* [Leics], one-third of the inhabitants were paupers, more than one-fifth of the houses stood empty and there was not enough work in the place to properly employ one-third of the weavers.

At *Manchester* the baker was more and more surprised at the number of people who bought halfpenny worths of bread . . . the linen draper told how new clothes were out of the question, and they bought only remnants and patches, to mend the old ones.

What would happen to the tradesmen if unemploy-
-ment continued?

In his *Survey of London Labour and London Poor*, published in 1851, Henry Mayhew reported the words of a man, who had been unemployed for three years, about how he managed. He had seven children and his wife was a washerwoman.

"We've known what it was sometimes to go without bread and coals in the depth of winter . . . . I have known us to sit several days and not have more than 6d. to feed and warm the whole of us for the day. We'll buy half a loaf; that'll be 4½d. or sometimes 5d., and then we had a 1d. for coals . . . we had to work hard to keep the children warm at all."

UNEMPLOYMENT IN THE LANCASHIRE COTTON TOWNS

During the American Civil War no cotton was sent to the Lancashire mills. The result was widespread unemployment among the workers. A woman from Clitheroe in Lancashire described the consequences in her diary in 1864:

The mill I work in was stopped all last winter, which time I had 3/- per week allowed by the relief committee which barely kept me alive. . . . . I have earned a 1/- a day this last month and there are many like me. My clothes and bedding is wearing out fast and I have no means of getting any more as what wages I get hardly keep me after paying rent, rates and firing.

Would you write a diary in such difficult times?
A London visitor to Blackburn in Lancashire also wrote about the distress in 1864:

Passing through another street I saw a woman busily engaged at an ironing board . . . . I asked her if she had regular employment in ironing.

"No sir, I wish I had", she answered. "It is nine or ten months now since I had regular work. I have been scraping a living together, though, by odd jobs and . . . I have been able to pawn things that I had by me and when things came very bad, I sold the pawn tickets, but now I have nothing left but the dress and I am going to sell it."

. . . With all it was the same fate — savings spent, credit exhausted, the pawn-
shop or the auction room, and last of all the terrible alternative — starvation or relief. One small street I found occupied entirely by the work people employed at one mill, which had been stopped more than 12 months ago. Every family had passed through the last winter without wages . . . some of them were lying four or five to a bed, others on bundles of straw.

Why do you think people were so afraid of asking for relief? How are the unemployed, the old and sick helped today?

The Relief of the Poor

WORKHOUSES

After 1834 fit people who sought help had to go into a workhouse, which was supported by the local rates. The conditions inside were deliberately harsh. Families were separated on admittance and, generally, people saw the workhouse as the last resort. Frederick Engels described the Manchester Workhouse in 1844:

> Manchester's "Poor Law Bastille". It is built on a hill, like a citadel, and from behind its high walls and battlements looks down threateningly upon the working class district below.

Why does he refer to it as a Bastille?

HELP FROM THE CHURCH

The churches and chapels also played a large part in helping the poor. The Rev Mantle, of Deptford Weslyan Medical Mission, received the following request. Can you translate it?

> Please Mr. Mantle will you give me a little releaf I ham holy a wider and got four little children to keap and I have to pool a barrow to London and back before I hern a loft of bread from Mrs. Kemp 5 Rouley Street Deptford.

A LONDON WORKHOUSE, 1871

Not all workhouses were so grim in appearance. Taine visited St Luke's workhouse:

> This one contains 500-600 old people, children who have been deserted . . . men and women out of employment (the smallest number) . . . . We went over 60-80 rooms . . . washhouse, brewery, bakehouse, shops for carpentry, for shoe-making, for oakum (rope) picking, rooms for the old men, rooms for the old women . . . all seemed sufficiently clean and healthy.

Find out where your workhouse was. The one in Bromley in Kent now forms part of Farnborough Hospital and several of the original buildings can still be seen.

VOLUNTARY HELP

Official help was aided, as it is today, by various charities. These often provided the poor with food or fuel. You could buy tickets from some charities which you would then give to people in need. The Editor of the *Bromley Record* advised his readers during the winter of 1870:

> ... those who could afford it will do well to carry a few tickets with them to give away to the needy.

These tickets were then used by the poor people at a soup kitchen run by volunteers in a local hall.

Edwin Waugh, a northern writer, described a soup kitchen in Accrington, Lancashire in 1862:

> In Accrington, broth was made in cauldrons over open fires in the market place by a group known as "the liberal women".

Deptford, c.1900. Many believed that the large number of public houses was a basic cause of poverty. This photograph shows the ones opposite the Deptford Weslyan Central Hall.

And he described breakfast for the poor in Preston, Lancashire, in the same year:

> Entering the yard, we found the wooden sheds crowded with people ... all ages from white haired men, bent with years, to eager childhood — 500 people breakfast in the sheds alone, every day ... it opens at five in the morning and there is always a crowd waiting to get in.

Forty years later soup kitchens were still needed in Deptford, London. Estimate how many people this might serve:

> Recipe for 1 day's soup — 2500 quarts
> 4 bullocks heads
> ½ cwt. of bones
> ½ cwt. shins of beef
> 1½ cwt. oatmeal
> ¼ ton of beans
> ¼ ton of vegetables
> 18 packets of herbs
> 18 bottles of Worcester sauce
> 1 bar of salt
> (From the First Report of the Deptford Weslyan Medical Mission)

Why do you think many people felt that the poor should be given tickets, clothes or food rather than money? Look in your local newspapers and try to find examples of charities. Look in your town for almshouses, hospitals and hostels for the poor as well.

Shops and Shopping

THE SHOPS IN A SMALL MARKET TOWN

Until the middle of the nineteenth century many shopkeepers were closely involved in either the growing or the manufacture of the goods they sold. Many had apprentices working for them, some of whom lived in. In the following list from Bagshaw's *Directory of Kent* you can see the range of trades, professions and shopkeepers in a small market town of under 5,000 people. Divide them into those connected with food, clothing, building and transport. Which of them would have had shops?

Bromley, Kent, 1847

Hotels, inns and taverns	(15)
Beerhouses	(10)
Attorneys	(2)
Auctioneers and estate agents	(2)
Bakers	(5)
Blacksmiths	(3)
Booksellers, stationers	(2)
Boot and shoemakers	(10)
Bricklayers	(4)
Butchers	(4)
Cabinet Makers	(3)
Carpenters	(3)
Chemists and druggists	(2)
Coal dealers	(2)
Corn dealers	(3)
Insurance offices	(4)
Glass & china dealers	(2)
Grocers and tea dealers	(9)
Hairdressers	(2)
Ironmongers	(3)
Linen drapers	(4)
Milliners and dressmakers	(5)
Plumbers, glaziers & painters	(4)
Printers	(2)
Saddlers & Harness makers	(2)
Shopkeepers (general)	(10)
Straw hat makers	(3)
Tailors & drapers	(10)
Tallow chandlers	(2)
Wheelwrights	(3)
Whitesmiths & bellhangers	(2)

With the coming of the railway, goods could be transported much more quickly and cheaply. Factory-produced goods became more readily available and the smaller shops came to face competition from larger shops and stores.

◀ *A Bromley ironmonger's, c. 1890. List the range of products displayed for sale.*

A directory advertisement of ▶ '1877. Look up the words which are unfamiliar to you and then suggest what each of the nine shops might have sold.

London has always contained a large number of expensive shops. Much was done to tempt the customer by advertisements and by window displays, as this extract from Knight's *Cyclopaedia of London 1851* shows:

> The furnishing ironmonger sets off his polished grates, fenders, candlesticks, etc. to the best advantage; the cabinet maker, with his French polished mahogany and his chintz coloured cotton furniture doing his best to tempt the passer by; the tobacconist displays his elegant snuff boxes, cigar cases, meerschaums and hookahs [pipes]; the perfumer decks his window with waxen ladies looking ineffably sweet.

Find out which are the oldest shops and stores in your town. You will find old trade directories, guides and advertisements useful. What advantage do modern shops have in advertising their goods?

For many of the poor, shops like those in London were only for window-gazing. Throughout the century the poor had to buy as cheaply as possible. Charles Knight in 1851 described the streets in London where they bought their necessities:

> In no other parts of London is the use of cellar-shops so conspicuous as in Monmouth Street. Every house has its cellar, to which access is gained by a flight of stairs from the open street, and every cellar has a shop, mostly for the sale of second-hand boots and shoes, which are ranged round the margin of the entrance, while countless children — noisy, dirty, are loitering within and without.
>
> In White-horse Street, Drury Lane . . . a small street is occupied almost entirely by open shops or stalls belonging to "piece brokers", who purchase old garments, and cut out from them such pieces as may be sound enough to patch other garments.

Monmouth Street still has street stalls today. Why did cellars make unsuitable shops?

23

Markets

Most towns had at least one market in the nineteenth century. Today the central market area may have been built on. Can you suggest why?

SHEFFIELD MARKET

Market day was a popular event, not only for buying and selling, but also simply for looking, as this popular song about Sheffield Market indicates:

> Next the market place survey when round
>   comes market day,
> And there such sights you'll see that
>   with me you will agree
> That Sheffield's a wonderful town, O.
> Lots of stalls against the walls;
> Make your rambles through the shambles,
> Beef and mutton, stuff a glutton;
> Butchers cry; who will buy?
> Dogs and asses, pretty lasses,
> If you gain Campo Lane,
> Neville's Ale, bright and pale,
> You will find it to your mind.

Can you guess what the shambles is from this verse? Several old cities, including York, have one.

CARNARVON MARKET, 1885

Town shopkeepers were often opposed to markets, because the goods sold in them were cheaper than in the shops. How can you tell this from the next extract taken from Abel Heywood's 1d. guide?

> The general market, held on Saturday, is plentifully supplied with butchers' meat, poultry, fruit, vegetables, eggs, and various kinds of agricultural produce, all excellent in quality, and sold at moderate rates. The butchers' market is well stocked, and numbers of small shop-keepers and quarrymen, from the neighbouring hamlets, buy eagerly and retail [sell] the same day at large profits. Many of these transfers of good things are effected at stalls, or on seats outside the buildings, in order to avoid the tolls.

What does the last sentence mean?

Whitby Market, by Frank Sutcliffe (1853-1941). He was renowned for the detail in his photographs. Note the goods which are for sale, and the dress of the people. The market hall is in the background.

SMITHFIELD MARKET, LONDON

Large cities, such as London, had several specialist markets. Charles Knight vividly describes the live-stock market at Smithfield, London, in 1851:

> There are two great thoroughfares by which cattle are brought to London — from the North by Highgate Archway, and from the Eastern Counties by White-chapel Road; large numbers are also brought by the various railways. They reach the outskirts of London on Sunday; about 9 o'clock in the evening they are driven into the city, and continue arriving in Smithfield from that hour until the morning. In this large irregular area, comprising about 3½ acres, enclosed by houses . . . . The drovers are furnished with torches to enable them to distinguish the marks on the cattle, to put the sheep into pens, and to form the beasts into "droves" . . . . The lowing of the oxen, the tremulous cries of the sheep, the barking of dogs, the rattling of sticks on the heads and bodies of the animals, the shouts of the drovers, and the flashing about of the torches, present altogether a wild and terrific combination.

How would the scene change when all the animals were brought to Smithfield by rail? Look out for green roads across country, along which the animals were driven and also for the various inn signs which remind us of this, e.g. Drover's Arms.

DERBY CATTLE MARKET, 1866

Black's *Guide to Derbyshire* of 1866 described the cattle market:

> The new Cattle Market is approached from the town by a bridge over the canal and from the other by a fine bridge over the river Derwent; and by new roadways which have been constructed. A siding for cattle has been made close to the market by the Midland Railway Company, and every possible convenience for farmers, dealers, and the public, has been provided.

Why do you think the new cattle market was well situated?

COUNTRY MARKETS

In most rural counties markets were the means by which farmers could meet to sell their animals and their produce. Knight's Suffolk Almanack for 1875 lists those convenient for Suffolk farmers.

Weekly corn markets

Bury	— Wed.	Halesworth	— Tue.
Beccles	— Fri.	Harleston	— W.
Bungay	— Thu.	Ipswich	— Tue.
Braintree	— Wed.	Maldon	— Tue.
Brandon	— Thu.	Mildenhall	— Fri.
Clare	— Mon.	Newmarket	— Tue.
Cambridge	— Sat.	Norwich	— Sat.
Chelmsford	— Fri.	Saxmundham	— Wed.
Colchester	— Sat.	Stowmarket	— Thur.
Diss	— Fr.	Stradbroke	— M.
Eye	— M.	Sudbury	— Th.
Framlingham	— Sat.	Woodbridge	— Th.
Hadleigh	— M.		

How many towns in your area had markets then? Do they still have them?

It is difficult to imagine the effect that the railway had upon Victorian England. This was because of the speed and the all-weather travelling which was now possible. Thomas Carlyle wrote:

> I perceive railways have set all the Towns of Britain a-dancing. Reading is coming up to London. Basingstoke is going down to Gosport or Southampton, Dumfries to Liverpool and Glasgow . . .

5,130 miles of track had been laid by 1850.

BROMLEY, BEFORE AND AFTER THE RAILWAY

While the major towns had a station, several smaller ones had not. It was only in 1858 that the railway came to Bromley, Kent. Before that, a local author had described the town:

> . . . it may be termed old-fashioned; a fair specimen of a small town in the old coaching days, but wanting [lacking] the coaches and every fourth man you meet to be an ostler . . . coaches passed through every hour . . . but the railway having absorbed nearly all the traffic, has rendered the Town of late years, one of the worst to get to or from, of any at the same distance from London: this state of things will shortly be altered . . .

Why do you think that the railway had virtually ended the long-distance coach traffic between London (via Bromley) and Dover, a distance of seventy miles?

A Bromley train and omnibus timetable, 1860. Look at the times of the trains and the fares. What sort of people would be able to travel to London daily by train? Note the horse-drawn omnibus which took passengers to the station.

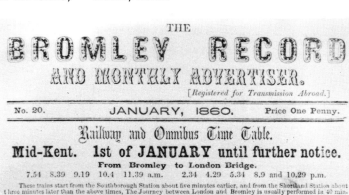

THE

BROMLEY RECORD

AND MONTHLY ADVERTISER.

[*Registered for Transmission Abroad.*]

No. 20.   JANUARY, 1860.   Price One Penny.

Railway and Omnibus Time Table.

Mid-Kent.   1st of JANUARY until further notice.

From Bromley to London Bridge.

7.54 8.39 9.19 10.4 11.39 a.m.   2.34 4.29 5.34 8.9 and 10.29 p.m.

These trains start from the Southborough Station about five minutes earlier, and from the Shortland Station about three minutes later than the above times, The Journey between London and Bromley is usually performed in 40 min.

From London Bridge to Bromley

7.50 8.10 9.10 and 10.30 a.m.   1.30 3.30 4.40 5.40 7.0 and 9.30 p.m.

NOTE.—*The 9.19 and 10.4 Up Trains, and the 4.40, and 5.40 Down Trains have no Third Class.   All the Sunday Trains have Third Class Carriages.*

From Bromley.   SUNDAYS.   **From London Bridge.**

10.4 a.m. 2.24 7.19 & 10.14 p.m. | 9.10 a.m. 1.30 6.15 & 9.15 p.m.

SINGLE JOURNEY.   **Fares**   RETURN.

First cl. 1s.6d; second cl. 1s,3d; third cl.10d. | First cl. 2s.3d; second cl. 1s.9d; third cl. 1s. 3d.

Omnibuses run between Bromley and Seven Oaks as follows.—From *Seven Oaks* (Dorset Arms and Crown Hotel) to meet the 10.4 a.m. and 5.34 p.m. Up Trains from Bromley Station; returning from Bromley on the arrival of the 10.30 a.m. and 4.40 p.m. Down Trains. On *Sundays* the Omnibus will meet the 9.10 a.m Down, and the 7.19 p.m. Up Trains.

FOWNES'S OMNIBUS will run to and from *Keston and Bromley Railway Station*, taking to the 9.19 11.39 4.29 and 8.9 Up Trains, *and from the 9.10 1.30 4.40 and 7.0 Down Trains, Week Days.   Sundays, to the 10.4 2.24 and 7.19 Up, and from the 9.10, 1.30 and 9.15 Down Trains, till further notice.*

PAWLEY'S OMNIBUS will leave St. Mary Cray at 8.15 a.m. Orpington at 8.22 a.m. to meet the 9.19 Up train from Bromley Station; returning on the arrival of the 1.30 p.m. from London Bridge.   Also from Cray at 3.30 to meet the 4.29 Up train returning on the arrival of the 5.40 Down.   Sundays, to meet the 10.4 a.m and 7.19 p.m. Up trains returning on the arrival of the 9.10 a.m. and 6.15 p.m. Down train.

An Omnibus to the Bromley Station, will leave Sundridge every morning. at 8.0 a.m., Brasted, 8.5, a.m, and Westerham, 8.20 a.m., (Sundays excepted), arriving at Bromley Station in time for the 10.4 a.m., for London.   Returning on the arrival of the 4.40, p.m. Train from London Bridge.   Fares, Inside 3s., Outside, 2s 6d.

No wonder there was rejoicing and hope when in May 1858 the railway finally arrived in Bromley. The *Bromley Record* reported:

A large crowd assembled on Martin's Hill to witness the departure of the first train [to London].

When was the station first opened in your town?

Between 1841 and 1861 Bromley's population grew very slowly, but look at the later increases. Note that a second station was opened in 1878.

Bromley's population 1861-1891

1861	5,505
1871	10,674
1881	15,154
1891	21,684

Compare your town's population. Did it rise with the coming of the railway? By 1891 a large number of Bromley people were working in London — Bromley had become a suburb.

THE SUBURB OF CROYDON

James Thorne described Croydon, 10 miles south of London, in 1878. (In 1871 the population of Croydon was 55,652.)

Croydon has eight railway stations and over 300 trains are despatched daily . . . . Lecture rooms, shops with showy plate glass windows, and joint-stock banks in the latest architecture mode are all occupying all the available sites in the leading thoroughfares. Monotonous streets and lines of villas are fast encircling the town, the neighbourhood of which being pleasant and picturesque, and within easy reach of the city, is a favourite residence for men of business who may be seen flocking to the morning trains in surprising numbers.

What advantages did Croydon have? Do you think that Thorne entirely approved of the changes?

BAD EFFECTS OF THE RAILWAYS

The railway attracted new residents and led to an increase in building. But, at the same time, there was some concern that new lines and stations displaced poor families, whose homes were destroyed. In London, new housing was rarely provided for such people and the poor often moved into already densely populated areas where the rent was cheap. There was also concern about the effect the railways had on the landscape. John Wilson described in 1878 how the view of Ludgate Hill and St Paul's had been spoiled.

The aggregate disfigurement of the metropolis [city] by the London

Chatham and Dover Railway Company, particularly by its viaducts and its bridges is very great. . . . That viaduct has utterly spoiled one of the finest street views in the metropolis; and is one of the most unsightly objects ever constructed, in any such situation anywhere in the world.

Compare this description with the picture on page 3.

Find out what your station replaced. Do we still view Victorian bridges and viaducts as Wilson did? How will the changes made in our time be viewed in years to come?

—Travel by Road, River and Sea

The 1830s saw not only the steam locomotive but also the steam ship (often combined with sail). However, as well as being the age of steam, the nineteenth century was the age of the horse, for the railway only put an end to long-distance coach traffic. Within the urban areas and over short distances, horse-drawn traffic — for goods and for people — increased as the population grew.

CARRYING GOODS BY ROAD

Carriers travelled within towns and to the neighbouring villages two or three times a week, with their horse-drawn vans, wagons and carts. Kelly's *Post Office Directory for Kent*, 1870, listed the carriers between Maidstone and Chatham:

> Carriers to
> CHATHAM. How, from his house, Earl Street Tues; Thurs; Sat; at 10 A.M.; Douch from the "Star" Mon; Tues; Thurs; and Sat; at 3 P.M.; Larking from Pudding Lane, Tues; Thurs; and Sat.

In all, eighty-seven places were served by carriers from Maidstone in 1870.

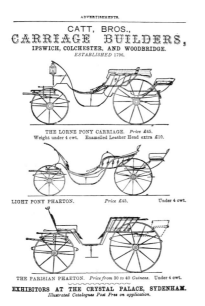

PASSENGER VEHICLES

By 1870 each major city had a wide variety of passenger vehicles on the roads. Baedeker's guide for London of 1885 told what was available there:

> *Cabs.* When the traveller is in a hurry, and his route does not coincide with that of an omnibus, he had better at once engage a cab . . . . The four-wheelers, which are small and uncomfortable, hold four persons inside, while a fifth can be accommodated beside the driver. The two-wheeled cabs, called Hansoms . . . have seats for two persons only and drive at a quicker rate. The driver's seat is at the

STEAM BOATS AT GRAVESEND

Charles Knight, writing in 1854, described Gravesend:

> The year 1834 witnessed the end of sailing packets, they were killed by steam . . . . In 1833 the number of persons conveyed [to Gravesend] had risen to 290,000 a year. After that came, in succession, the formation of the Terrace Pier, the establishment of the Star Company, in opposition to the Diamond or Old Company; the building of the pier at Rosherville, the rebuilding of the Terrace Pier, and the sale of it to the Corporation, and the changes effected by the opening of the Blackwall Railway. By the year 1840 the steam boat passengers had reached a million annually. In 1844 a million and a half were conveyed in four months!

◀ *One of several carriage advertisements from a Suffolk Directory. Who might have bought the ones shown?*

back so he drives over the heads of the passengers inside. Orders are communicated through a small trap door in the roof. There are now upwards of 9,600 cabs in London employing about 17,000 horses.

Fares 1/- up to two miles.

Omnibuses of which there are more than 100 lines, [run] from eight in the morning till midnight. They are now mainly in the hands of the London General Omnibus Company. In view of comfort these vehicles leave much to be desired. Fares 1d. to 6d.

The Eider, 1877. Note the range of ports which were served by the ship, and suggest the type of goods which might have been carried.

Each omnibus route had its own name and colour:

> Atlas. Light green. St. John's Wood, Oxford Street, Camberwell Gate — every 10 minutes.

In 1870 tramways were introduced in London. The "cars are comfortable and the fares moderate". They were run by various companies, and the tram was one of the main reasons for the spread of the towns and cities. Why do you think this was?

THE LIFE OF A LONDON OMNIBUS DRIVER

Henry Mayhew described the work of omnibus drivers in 1851:

> Their work is exceedingly hard — Most of them enter the yard at a quarter to eight in the morning, and must see that their horses and carriages are in a proper condition for work. They start at 8.30 and some are on their box till after midnight. [One told me that] "I have never had any rest but a few minutes except every other Sunday and then only two hours. It's hard work for the horses — the starting after stopping is the hardest work for them, it's such a terrible strain. I've felt for the poor things on a wet night, with a bus full of big people . . . . I must keep exact time at every place where a time-keeper's stationed. Not a minute's excused — there's a fine for the least delay . . . . Every horse in our stables has one day's rest in every four; but it's no rest for the driver."

This man earned 34s. a week.

List as many occupations as you can which were based upon the horse, e.g. corn dealer, stable boy.

Holidays

Cheaper and quicker travel on the railway, the decrease in the length of the working day and the introduction of public holidays all led to the growth of holidays.

BRIGHTON, 1885

Before the railway, Brighton had been a wealthy resort for the rich of London. By 1885 this had changed, as Abel Heywood shows:

> Day trips, cheap trains, excursion trains, and season tickets, have made Brighton a marine suburb of London. The aristocrat visits it . . . for the purpose of patronising the "Age" [a coach] and "doing the road" in the style of our coaching fathers.
>
> The merchant takes his family to London-super-Mare for the season, and returns night and morning per [by] express. The clerk revels in the thought of a periodical sight of the ocean.
>
> The workman thinks of taking his wife to Brighton and back for 3/-. This also tempts the country visitor. So we all go to Brighton and this is what we see:- a frank, open, smiling town, with handsome terraces, a broad esplanade, a royal freak of a palace [the Pavilion], two inviting piers, white cliffs in the distance and a glorious sea.

Note the range of visitors and Brighton's attractions.

BLACKPOOL, LANCASHIRE, 1885

By the 1880s Blackpool was established as the leading seaside town of the North-West. Abel Heywood wrote:

> There was a time when the trip to the seaside was a luxury of the rich, but all that has now changed. Nowadays, to visit the seaside is regarded as an annual necessity — the summer exodus from inland manufacturing towns numbering hundreds of thousands. Its *attractions* — It possesses innumerable lodging houses, stores and first class hotels, many fine public gardens and places of resort, handsome public baths, commodious theatres, and, in fact, everything that tends to make up a model of a seaside town, catering for the recreation and amusement of the million.

Why do you think Blackpool became so popular to those from the inland towns?

Of course, towns had to spend heavily on improvements. Blackpool's promenade cost £60,000 and the pier was built as an attraction. Heywood described the North Pier in 1885:

Central Beach, Blackpool in the 1880s. You can see the North Pier, promenade and the newly built hotels with their gardens. Today the gardens and most of houses have been replaced by the amusement les of the Golden Mile.

THE SEASIDE OCCUPATIONS OF MARGATE

The census of 1841 gives the seaside occupations of Margate. There were also ninety-six lodging house-keepers.

Bazaar assistants	18
Milliners	15
Coachmen	14
Bathers	13
Ticket porters	10
Waiters	9
Boarding house keepers	5
Strawbonnet makers	4
Bonnetmakers	3
Donkey keepers	2
Eating houses	2
Bun sellers	1
Coffee House keepers	1
Ginger beer maker	1
Sells fruit	1

The finest marine parade in Europe. It is 1,850 feet long and possesses a pierhead with a spacious Indian pavilion and shops, refreshment rooms and band kiosk. Also steamers and sailing boats.

Many more must have worked in the holiday trade than the census shows, judging by Charles Knight's description of 1854:

> Italian organ boys, fortune-telling gypsies, bears, and monkeys, a camel, hurdigurdies [organs], conjurers, tumblers, fish-hawkers, shrimp sellers, criers of fruit and vegetables, match venders, sellers of corn plaster, and the town bellman keep the Fort — the choicest part of Margate — alive and ringing from eight in the morning till nine at night.

A WEEK IN MARGATE, 1886

Thirty years later a visitor to Margate showed how he had "taken home change out of a £5 note".

	£ s d
Journey there by rail	4. 3
Journey back by boat	5. 3
Board and lodging	1.11. 6
Entertainment and excursions	2. 2.11
Shopping	8. 0
Church donations	1. 6
Royal Sea Bathing Infirmary (gift)	5. 0
Other gifts	1. 6
TOTAL	4.19.11

Where do you think the visitor came from?

Not everyone chose the seaside for their holiday. Find other examples of places which became popular. Directories and advertisements will be useful.

Sport

DERBY DAY, EPSOM, SURREY, 1864

With more leisure time, sport became more available to wider numbers. Big race meetings attracted large crowds. Note the various forms of transport used to get to the Derby at Epsom. Which would the "better off" have used? The extract comes from Black's *Guide to Surrey*.

> No European country can match the spectacle presented by Epsom on Derby Day. The railways bring down their thousands, while from every part of the metropolis and the surrounding country the roads which converge towards the great centre attraction are crowded with "four in hands", barouches, phaetons, gigs, chaises, carts, omnibuses, stage coaches, trucks and equestrians. Upwards of **100,000** persons assemble to take their part in this grand national gala.

▲

Racing on Epsom Downs, an etching from Black's Guide of 1864. Compare this with the written account in the Guide.

CRICKET

Cricket had long been our major summer sport and by the end of the nineteenth century the county championship had been firmly established. The *Boys' Own Paper* of 1893 described the Surrey v. Notts match played at The Oval on August Bank Holiday, 1892:

> In the Bank Holiday match when the eleven [Surrey] were without their usual wicketkeeper and suffered accordingly, there were 63,763 visitors to the Oval. It was a great contest, well-fought to the end, and cheered to the echo by the crowd.

Why was such a large crowd able to be there? Look in Wisden's Almanack for details of other matches.

The following advertisement appeared in the *Bromley Record* in June 1867. Joseph Wells was a Kent County cricketer and the father of the novelist H.G. Wells.

> Cricket! Cricket! Cricket!
> Joseph Wells has an excellent selection of all Goods requisite for the noble game, are of first class quality and moderate prices. His cane-handled Bats specially selected by himself are acknowledged to be unsurpassed in the trade. Youths' Bats of all sizes, &c., &c., at his
> OLD ESTABLISHED CHINA & GLASS WAREHOUSE,
> High Street, Bromley, Kent.

Aston Villa F.C. 1886-87. During this season they ▶ *gained their record victory 13-0 v. Wednesbury Old Athletic in the First Round of the F.A. Cup. The club was formed in 1874.*

FOOTBALL

Professional football was introduced in England in 1885 and three years later the Football League was formed. Rothman's *Football Year Book* gives us the original twelve members. Note that all the teams came from industrial towns. Why was this? Find out when your local team was founded.

1888 Football League founded —
Accrington, Aston Villa, Blackburn

Rovers, Bolton Wanderers, Burnley, Derby County, Everton, Notts County, Preston North End, Stoke, West Bromwich Albion, Wolverhampton Wanderers.

The F.A. Cup was first introduced in the season 1871-72. The competition in 1898-99 took the following course:

Wisden for cricket and almanacks, annuals and club histories for football will provide useful information. Find out from your local newspaper whether your favourite sport was being played in this period. Do they still play in their original place?

F.A. CHALLENGE CUP COMPETITION 1898–99

First Round

Everton v Jarrow	3 1
Nottm. Forest v Aston V.	2 1
Sheffield U. v Burnley	2 2, 2 1
Preston N.E. v Grimsby T.	7 0
W.B.A. v South Shore	8 0
Heanor T. v Bury	0 3
Liverpool v Blackburn R.	2 0
Glossop v Newcastle U.	0 1
Notts C. v Kettering	2 0
New Brompton v Southampton	0 1
Woolwich Arsenal v Derby C.	0 6
Bolton W. v Wolverhampton W.	0 0, 0 1
Small Heath v Manchester C.	3 2
Stoke v Sheffield W.	2 2, 2 0
Newton Heath v Tottenham H.	1 1, 3 5
Bristol C. v Sunderland	2 4

Second Round

Everton v Nottm. Forest	0 1

Sheffield U. v Preston N.E.	2 2, 2 1
W.B.A. v Bury	2 1
Liverpool v Newcastle U	3 1
Notts C. v Southampton	0 1
Derby C. v Wolverhampton W.	2 1
Small Heath v Stoke	2 2, 1 2
Tottenham H. v Sunderland	2 1

Third Round

Nottm. Forest v Sheffield U.	0 1
W.B.A. v Liverpool	0 2
Southampton v Derby C.	1 2
Stoke v Tottenham H.	4 1

Semi-Final

Sheffield U. v Liverpool	2 2, 3 4 4, 1 4 0 0, 5 1 0
Derby C. v Stoke	6 3 1

Final 1898–99: Derby C. 1 Sheffield U. 4

[1] Abandoned, crowd encroached on field. [2] At Nottingham. [3] At Bolton. [4] At Manchester. [5] At Derby. [6] At Wolverhampton.

Again, note the teams. Where did most of them come from?

Education

For much of the nineteenth century education was neither compulsory nor free, and until 1870 it was undertaken by voluntary groups. The growing population of the towns and cities posed severe problems. The education of the poor was largely in the hands of the British and Foreign School Society (Nonconformist) and the larger National Society (Church of England). Look out for old school buildings with plaques inscribed "British school" or "National school".

A late Victorian schoolroom, recreated at St John's ▶ *House, Coten End, Warwick, a branch of the County Museum service. What features are similar to and different from your classroom?*

A present-day class being taught at St John's. Note ▶ *the slates, continuous benches and the discipline of the time.*

ST JOHN'S SCHOOL, PENGE

In Penge, Surrey, a National school was founded in 1837. The school log book kept by the head teacher in the 1860s includes the following:

> The Home lessons very imperfectly done today. The class is kept in during the Dinner hour to reproduce them.
>
> Tripp and Hunt are sent home for irregular attendance.
>
> Field is sent home until his money is brought for a week.
>
> Edmund Wright detected in a falsehood, about stealing from Mr. Warn's orchard. Publicly flogged.

Parents were charged 2d a week for their child's education. As you can see, sometimes the school had difficulty in collecting this money.

If your school is an old one, try to draw a plan of the building as it was, and look for any old school magazines which may have survived. It is more likely that your school will not be old. In this case, try to find from old guides and directories the schools that did exist in the nineteenth century.

SCHOOL BOARDS

Following an enquiry into the state of education, an Education Act was passed in 1870, under which school boards (committees) were to be formed if there were insufficient school places in an area. The school board was elected by the ratepayers and could levy rates for elementary education.

Holt's *Guide to Sutton* gives the following details about the Sutton, Surrey School Board in 1896:

Board room — West Street. Clerk's Office — 138 High Street
Chairman — Rev. H.W. Turner
Vice Chairman — Mr. A.T. Williams
Members — Rev. J. Jones, Messrs. Carpenter, Orton, Rogers and Stevens.
Attendance Officer — Mr. Wm. Cutts, Manor Lane.
Master of New Town Boys — Mr. T. Watson, Manor Lane.
West Street Boys — Mr. Cooke, West Street.
Crown Road Boys — Mr. Adams, Oakhill Road.
Mistress of New Town Girls — Miss Brown
New Town Infants — Miss Anderson
Crown Road Girls — Miss Priestley
Crown Road Infants — Miss Jarman
West Street Infants — Mrs. Watson

What would the Attendance Officer do? Many new schools were built by the school boards. Look out for them in your area and see how the boys and girls often had separate entrances and playgrounds.

Inspectors regularly visited every school and several boards encouraged the children by awarding prizes for merit and medals for attendance.

GRAMMAR SCHOOLS

Some towns had grammar schools, some of which had been founded in Tudor times. Two are mentioned in *A Pictorial History of Lancashire* in 1844.

Lancaster. A school was built to contain 120 boys in two stories, on one of which writing and arithmetic are taught, and on the other classes. There is a small library attached. The master is paid £70 per annum.
Blackburn. The Free Grammar School was founded by Queen Elizabeth . . . . This school is "free to the world". The master's salary is £90. There is a small entrance fee.

Why should the latter be "free to the world" and still charge an entrance fee?

A LONDON SECONDARY SCHOOL, 1883

Molly Hughes attended the North London Collegiate School where the discipline was very strict under a severe head, Miss Buss.

Apart from the permanent rules . . . almost every day a new one appeared in a corridor in large sprawling home-made lettering — such as: 'Broken needles must not be thrown on the floor'. Every book had to be covered (a different colour for each subject). No girl might bring a pen to school (was this to avoid ink-stains?). We were forbidden to get wet on our way to school, to walk more than three in a row, to drop a pencil box, leave a book at home, hang a boot bag by only one loop, run down the stairs, speak in class.

Police and Prisons

Crime in the major towns and cities was a real problem in the early nineteenth century, but many people were willing to accept it rather than have a uniformed police force. However, Sir Robert Peel was eventually able to get through Parliament the Metropolitan Police Act in 1829. This act introduced uniformed police (bobbies or peelers) in London and marked the beginning of our modern police force.

PRISONS

Large cities contained several prisons and each county was required to have one. The Governor's Record Book of 1842 tells us the following about the County Gaol at Maidstone, Kent:

NEWGATE PRISON, LONDON, 1851

One of the most infamous of London's prisons was Newgate. Charles Knight felt that the building was quite unsatisfactory.

> Some things, however, still exist that are scarcely credible. The cells are unlighted and unwarmed; the prisoners consequently suffer from cold, and after they are shut up for the night the strong deprive the weak of their blankets and rugs, and scenes take place which baffle description. The food when given is not eaten in the presence of an officer; no knife or fork is allowed, only a spoon. . . . The number of prisoners who passed through the prison in 1848 was 3,436, of whom 2,797 were males, and 639 females.

Note the difference between the Maidstone and the Newgate extracts. The first is an official one written by the Governor, the second by a visitor. How can you tell the difference?

		Total number of prisoners
Michaelmas	1841	395
(Sept. 29)	1842	498
Number of prisoners committed during the course of the year		3,674
Prisoners employed:		
Hard labour		310
Other labour		34
Not employed		154
Cases of sickness during the year		1,330
Deaths		26

Work. Male prisoners sentenced to hard labour are employed at the treading wheels, at the manufacture of sacking, mat making, tailoring, shoe making and shoe mending. Male prisoners not sentenced to hard labour are employed at a capstan to raise water for the supply of the prison, also in gardening, white-washing, oakum picking, cleaning the prison and other general labour. Females sentenced to hard labour are employed at the treading wheels, washing, ironing and needlework, those who are not sentenced to hard labour are employed in cleaning the prison, picking oakum and needle-work.

Hours. The prisoner commences work at six in the morning and leaves work at half past five.

Roughly, what proportion of prisoners fell sick during 1842? What is the main difference between hard labour and general labour, and between men's and women's work?

Try to find out when and where your county gaol was built.

THE LONDON POLICE IN 1854

The *Pictorial Handbook to London* described some of the duties of the London police:

> The police are a body of men appointed to preserve order and apprehend offenders ... they act under the direction of two commissioners appointed by the Crown. They have power to suppress illegal fairs, unlicensed theatres, places used for baiting lions, bears, badgers, cocks, dogs, and other animals, gaming houses, to regulate the route and conduct of the drivers of carriages during the hours of Divine service and public procession.

What does this tell us about cruel sports?

DIFFICULT AREAS TO POLICE

The police force only developed outside London in the 1840s and '50s. In most towns and cities there were areas where the police would not patrol alone. Charles Dickens described a night journey with five armed police officers into the worst area of London in *Household Words* in 1851. He was impressed that the journey was possible; not that the police were armed. Liverpool also faced severe problems. The Commissioner of Police described the dock area of North Liverpool in 1846:

> Even if a man commits a disturbance it is folly for the police, two or three of them to attempt to take him in the neighbourhood, there must be a considerable force.

A page from the records of Huntingdon County Gaol. Note the age of the boy and the severity of the sentence.

Churches and Chapels

The Victorians were as interested in bringing Christianity to those at home as were their missionaries to those in other lands. Churches and chapels, and National and British schools were deliberately built in poor areas, and new churches were also built in the more prosperous suburbs.

Find out when the chapels and churches in your area were built. The directories will give you a list of them. Note the wide variety of chapels. The *Directory for Kent* for 1870 lists the following in Chatham:

> Chatham Church (St. Mary's)
> St. John's, Railway Street
> St. Paul's, New Road
> Garrison Church (for the dockyard and
>   naval barracks)
> Roman Catholic, Ordnance Place
> Independent Chapel, Clover Street
> Old General Baptist's Meeting House,
>   Hammond Hill
> Baptist Chapel, Clover Street
> Baptist Chapel, 52 High Street
> Wesleyan Chapel, James Street
> Congregational Chapel, Brook Street
> Salem Chapel, Rhode Street
> Wesleyan Chapel, Ordnance Place
> Bible Christian's Chapel, Union Street
> Primitive Methodist's Chapel, George
>   Street

CHURCHES IN KENT

At Bickley in Kent, George Wythes paid for the church to be put up on the estate that he had built. Kelly's *Post Office Directory for Kent* for 1870 contains the following:

> Bickley is studded with modern villas. The church of St. George, a handsome building of stone, with a lofty spire and a clock, was opened in 1864; . . . it is neatly pewed, and has accommodation for 820.

Bromley Baptist Church, erected in 1864 to serve the new population attracted by the railway (see page 27).

▼

BUILDING AND RESTORING CHURCHES

Many churches look much older than they are, because the Victorians liked to build in older styles, as this example, from Chamber's *Directory of Eastbourne of 1886* shows. St Saviour's, Eastbourne, Sussex was:

> A new church . . . built in 1882. It cost £15,000 and is built in the Gothic and early English style of about 1100 A.D.

In addition, the Victorians also restored or enlarged many churches. Look in your local church and note when alterations were made and see if there is a plaque to say who gave the money. John Wilson described the churches in Maidstone, Kent:

> St. Peter's Church — stood long in a state of neglect and dilapidation and was restored and enlarged in 1839.
> St. Philip's Church was built in 1858 and greatly altered in 1869.
> All Saint's has a new North memorial window to C. Mercer erected in 1864.

CHURCH ATTENDANCE

It would be misleading to suggest that the majority of people went to church or chapel in the nineteenth century . In 1851 a Religious Census was taken of all those attending church on a particular Sunday. It showed that on average only a third of the population attended. In Sheffield a second Religious Census was carried out in 1881.

	Population	Attendances	Number of churches and chapels
1851	135,000	43,000	70
1881	284,400	87,750	196

Some people attended church more than once on a Sunday. How might this give a false picture of total attendances? Was Sheffield above or below the national average?

The same church today. Note the house to the right on both photographs. To the left a School of Art was built at the end of the century, and a right of way still remains between the two buildings.

CEMETERIES

As the population grew, many existing graveyards became full. Land was purchased for new ones on the outskirts of towns. Wilson described the cemeteries in Birmingham in 1878:

> The general cemetery at Key Hill, comprises nearly 11 acres; was in great part excavated from rock, is tastefully laid out with walls and shrubberies, has a chapel in the centre, and contains many fine monuments. The Church of England cemetery, near this, was opened in 1848; comprises about nine acres, and has a beautiful church in the later English style with tower and spire. The city cemetery was recently formed at a cost of £75,000, comprises 105 acres.

Churchyards and cemeteries are well worth a visit, for a gravestone gives us information about a person or family. Many of the towns have now "caught up" with the cemeteries, so that they are now in built-up areas, not outside. This has also happened to isolation hospitals and asylums.

Changes in Five Towns

So far the emphasis has been upon growth and change. The last two sections look at the way in which six different towns and cities changed during the lives of many people.

BRISTOL IN 1885

Abel Heywood described the changes which had taken place in Bristol:

> Modern enterprise is fast destroying all traces of old Bristol. Its once narrow, crooked and antiquated looking streets are by degrees being displaced by spacious and handsome thoroughfares. Within the last ten years over a £¼m. have been raised by local rates, and expended in street improvements, and further extensive alterations are contemplated.

Note how the money for the street improvements was raised.

LLANDUDNO IN 1885

Some changes were even more dramatic. Blackpool, Fleetwood and Llandudno grew very quickly from villages into towns. Abel Heywood described the Welsh town:

> Before 1850 mainly a mining village, then developed by local landowner into one of the great watering places and fashionable seaside resorts. This occurred in 1849 when the villagers were informed that the Honourable E.M.L. Mostyn M.P. had instructed Mr. Lloyd of Ruthin to sell by auction in 176 lots, that part of Gladdoeth Estate consisting of the then projected, and now erected, new town of Llandudno.

Expensive hotels were built.

> There are nine crescents, or blocks of buildings of the first class all having sea frontage, and looking over a carriage drive and broad terrace walls of turf and fine gravel.

LEICESTER IN 1864

Leicester, too, saw many changes. Try to find out what was produced in Leicester's new factories. Where would the goods have been produced before this? Dr John Barclay spoke of Leicester in 1864:

> On all sides vast blocks of warehouses have arisen, while the development of new manufactures, or the substitution of steam machinery for hand labour has raised a forest of long factory chimneys. Twenty years and two months ago when taking my first survey of the town . . . I counted with difficulty 50 chimneys . . . now at nearly 250.

He then went on to describe one area of the city:

> The poor cricket ground has been entirely laid out in streets and is already pretty well built over. Beyond that there are miles of streets, which is called New Leicester — indeed a new town has risen up there, Brunswick Street, Curzon Street, Stanley Street, Cobden Street, running away into what, only a few years ago, were green fields and pastures.

Street names are often useful clues to dating a street or road. Find out who Cobden was.

Liverpool, 1836 and 1891. List as many changes as you can which have taken place, especially the improvements and the station and lines. What evidence of a railway can you find in the earlier map?

CHANGES IN MERTHYR, 1854-1870

Most of the people in Merthyr in South Wales worked in the huge Dowlais Iron Works, and its population grew very quickly. The town climbed 150 metres up the steep valley (in 4 kilometres). Charles Knight was very critical:

> Is there not justification for a little reproof of the wealthy men who possess the great works of the neighbourhood, that not one yard of sewer or drain exists in this town of 50,000 inhabitants? And the lamps in the streets, and the paving of the roads, and the sweeping of the mud, and the supplying of water — there is little to say that is creditable and we gladly escape it altogether.

How would these conditions affect the health of the people?

Eventually, a local board of health was formed which could levy rates. The town had improved considerably when Black's *Guide to Wales* was published in 1870:

> The populous town . . . was, until lately, a shapeless unsightly cluster of wretched dingy dwellings; but having in recent years undergone much improvement as well as extension, it now contains some regular, well built streets, a court-house, a market house, several elegant private residences, a large number of respectable shops, four churches and no fewer than 34 dissenting [non-conformist] chapels.

Change in Birmingham

Seeing a Victorian town hall or travelling from one of the main line stations, we rarely consider what they replaced. Birmingham in 1801 had 71,000 people, in 1851 233,000, in 1901 523,000. Here is an early nineteenth-century song which describes the changes which were beginning:

I can't find Brummagem (Birmingham)
Full 20 years or more have passed
Since I left Brummagem,
But I set out for home at last
to good old Brummagem.
But every place is altered so,
There's hardly a single place I know,
which fills my heart with grief and woe,
For I can't find Brummagem.

Amongst the changes we have got
In good old Brummagem,
They've made a market on the moat*
To sell the pigs in Brummagem
But that has brought us more ill-luck:
They've filled up poor old Pudding Brook,
Where in the mud I've often stuck,
Catching Jack-bannils [sticklebacks]
    near Brummagem.

I remember one John Growse,
A buckle-maker in Brummagem,
He built himself a country house
To be out of the smoke of Brummagem,
But though John's country house stands
    still,
The town itself has walked up hill;
Now he lives beside a smoky mill
In the middle of the streets of
    Brummagem.

*The moat which surrounded the site of the old manor house was filled in in 1816 to make way for Smithfield Market.

Are there any houses or streets in your town which are much older than the others? Try to find out when they were built.

Two views of Birmingham. The first shows Ann Street, the site of the Council House (or Town Hall) in the second picture. See how quickly change has come, for the statue of Sir Robert Peel, which can be seen in both photographs, was only unveiled in 1855. Compare the photographs with the written descriptions in this section. ▶

▼

BIRMINGHAM TOWN HALL, 1885

The second half of the century saw even more improvements. Abel Heywood described the new town hall:

> This is one of the finest public buildings in Birmingham, and is used for great town meetings and the celebrated Triennial [every three years] Musical Festivals. It is of the Corinthian order of architecture, the pillars which surround it being copied from the temple of Jupiter, at Rome. It is built of Anglesey marble and was commenced in 1832, completed in 1852 at a cost of nearly £50,000 . . .
>
> The Great Hall will accommodate sitting between 3,000 and 4,000 persons, but at great political and religious meetings; . . . as many as 10,000.

Has your town a Victorian town hall? Find out when it was built — it may have a foundation stone. Why were so many of them built on such a magnificent scale?

OTHER BUILDINGS IN BIRMINGHAM

Abel Heywood also commented on the Central Free Library in Birmingham:

> This noble building . . . consists of a reading room, a lending library, and a reference library. The first two were opened in 1864 and the latter in 1866 — It is one of the best reading rooms in the Kingdom. The library was built, and is supported out of the public rates.

Note that books were loaned free to the public.

Other buildings which were built or developed in Birmingham in the 1850s and '60s were:

1806	Public Offices — greatly extended 1861 and 1865
1854	New Street Station
1860	Temperance Hall
1869	New Courts, new Post Office, and two large banks

In the last twenty years Birmingham has seen extensive redevelopment and much of Victorian Birmingham has been destroyed. When were the Victorian buildings in your town built? Do they still exist? List the changes which have taken place in your town during (a) your memory, (b) that of your parents.

43

Places to Visit

Many fine Victorian buildings and streets have in the last twenty years been demolished. Fortunately, the planners are now realizing their importance. The following is a selection only.

1. MUSEUMS
    a) *London*
       The Museum of London contains a fine section on Victorian London.
       The Victoria and Albert Museum is the leading museum on the art and crafts of the past. This and other museum buildings in Exhibition Road are splendid examples of Victorian architecture.
    b) *York*
       The Castle Museum — has reconstructed shops and streets.
       The Railway Museum.
    c) *Bradford*
       Moorside Mills Industrial Museum.
    d) *Darlington*
       Railway Museum in North Road Railway Station.

2. STATIONS
    St Pancras, London, built in 1868 by Gilbert Scott.

3. MEMORIALS
    The Albert Memorial, London, 1861.
    The Scott Memorial, Edinburgh.

4. TOWN HALLS
    Rochdale, Manchester, Sheffield.

5. MUSIC AND ENTERTAINMENT
    Blackpool, Grand Theatre.
    Albert Hall, London (1871).

6. PUBLIC BUILDINGS
    Leeds — Corn Exchange (1861), Rochdale, Manchester and Sheffield Town Halls.

7. HOUSES
    Osborne House, Isle of Wight — belonged to Queen Victoria.

8. PIERS
    Eastbourne, North Pier, Blackpool.

9. STREETS
    Lord Street, Southport.

10. SEASIDE TOWNS
    Llandudno, Eastbourne, Fleetwood.

11. INDUSTRIAL TOWNS
    Preston, Bradford, Blackburn.

12. RAILWAY TOWNS
    Crewe, Darlington (both railway).

13. SPA TOWNS
    Harrogate, Leamington.

14. SUBURBS
    Beckenham, outskirts of Sheffield, Leicester and Nottingham.

Map of places mentioned in the text.

Glasgow

Lancaster
Fleetwood
Blackpool
Clitheroe
Preston
Accrington
Blackburn
York
Bolton
Leeds
Hull
Llandudno
Liverpool
Manchester
Salford
Birkenhead
Carnarvon
Crewe
Sheffield

Derby
Nottingham

Leicester
Birmingham
Hinckley

Stratford-on-Avon

Merthyr Tydfil
Ipswich

St. Albans
Cardiff
LONDON
Bristol
Swindon
Gravesend
Sutton
Margate
Epsom
Bromley
Chatham
Croydon
Maidstone
Dover

Brighton
Eastbourne

0 20 40 60 80 100
km

Difficult Words

aspidistra	a large indoor plant.
bobbies or peelers	members of the first police force founded by Sir Robert Peel in 1829.
broker	one who buys and sells for others.
calico	cotton cloth.
census	the official count of population. In England it has been taken every ten years from 1801, except for 1941.
cholera	a highly infectious and deadly disease. Known as King Cholera in the nineteenth century because it attacked both rich and poor alike.
court	space surrounded by houses.
dialist	maker of dials.
die sinker	an engraver of dies. Dies are tools used for making impressions, e.g. a die for stamping a coin.
domestic worker	one who works at home. The hand-loom weavers worked at home, as did many needleworkers.
Gothic	(early English) a style of architecture with high pointed arches. It followed the Norman style in the twelfth century.
Japanning	a glossy black varnish or lacquer; first used by the Japanese.
log book (school)	a daily diary kept by the head teacher of a school.
lustre	a shiny looking glaze on pottery.
Ordnance Survey	founded in 1801 and produces maps of all areas.
papier-mâché	paper mixed with water to make pulp and then pasted together and painted to look like varnished wood.
paupers	poor, usually living on poor relief or charity.
porter	a drink popular with London porters.
rates	money collected from householders to pay for local services.
School Board	the committee elected by the rate-payers who supervised the Board schools.
suburb	a place on the outskirts of a town from which most of the people travel in to the town or city to work.
villa	a house usually built for the more prosperous. You will see many old houses with villa in the name, e.g. Rosemary Villas, Crystal Palace Villas.

Money

Always look at what money and wages could buy rather than at what seem low prices to us. It is no use butter being 4p a pound if we only earn 50p a week.

Remember that there were 12 old pence (d) in a shilling (s) and 20 shillings to the pound. 6d was the equivalent of 2½p, a shilling (1/-) 5p.

Biographical Notes

-Books to Use-

BAEDEKER, Karl German publisher whose guides became famous. Extremely detailed and included good maps. Always in red covers.

BLACK, A.C. Another publisher of country, town and county guides. Nineteenth-century ones had green covers.

DICKENS, Charles Novelist. Many of his novels describe the lives of the poor in Victorian towns and cities.

GASKELL, Mrs She did much to bring to the reader the conditions in the cities of the North.

GRANVILLE, A.B. Born in Germany, and a doctor by profession.

GREENWOOD, J. Wrote several books exposing life among the poor in Victorian London.

HEYWOOD, A. Another publisher, this time of Penny guides.

HUGHES, M.V. Her four volumes of autobiography have become classics of their kind.

KELLY A publisher who concentrated on county and town directories. They are very detailed.

KNIGHT, C. An author and publisher who did much to bring knowledge to the people in the first part of the nineteenth century. In spite of his success, he died in poverty.

MAYHEW, H. A journalist whose articles for the press on the poor were published later in book form.

TAINE, H. A Frenchman who wrote the fascinating Notes on England based on a visit to England in 1861.

The Chartists Peter Searby, Longman "Then and There" series, 1967

Discovering Local History David Paul Titley, Allman, 1972

Edwin Chadwick, Poor Law and Public Health Watson, Longman "Then and There" series, 1969

Getting About in Towns Paul White, A. & C. Black, 1976

Law and Order. The Story of the Police John Dumpleton, A. & C. Black, 1970

Let's Use the Locality (teacher's handbook) Henry Pluckrose, Mills and Boon, 1971

London Life and the Great Exhibition, 1851 J.R.C. Yglesias, Longman "Then and There" series

Looking Around in Town and Country Philip Sauvain, F. Watts, 1975

People of the Past series, vol G Burton et al., OUP, 1968

Police and Prisons P.F. Speed, Longman "Then and There" series, 1968

Seen in Britain Henry Pluckrose, Mills and Boon, 1977

Towns and Town Life Alan Hammersley, Blandford, 1973

The Victorians Boswell Taylor (Ed), Hodder, 1977

Victorian and Edwardian Birmingham D. McCulla and Gray, Batsford, 1972

Victorian and Edwardian Bristol R. Winstone, Batsford, 1976

Victorian and Edwardian Cambridge F.A. Reeve, Batsford, 1971

Victorian and Edwardian City of London J. Howgego, Batsford, 1977

Victorian and Edwardian Edinburgh C.S. Minto, Batsford, 1976

Victorian People Stella Margetson, Batsford, 1977

A Victorian Sunday Jill Hughes, Wayland, 1972

Victorian Times John Shepherd (Ed), Mills and Boon, 1977

Victorian Times to the Second World War David Paul Titley, Allman, 1973

Molly Hughes's autobiography about Victorian London was first published in 1937 and has been recently re-issued. It is very readable.

A London Child of the 1870s M.V. Hughes, OUP, 1978

A London Girl of the 1880s M.V. Hughes, OUP, 1978

A London Home in the 1890s M.V. Hughes, OUP, 1978

Index